The
COTSWOLDS
Area of Outstanding Natural Beauty

Photography by Nick Turner
Written by Siân Ellis
Designed by Nick Darien-Jones

Published in Great Britain in 2016 on behalf of the
Cotswolds Conservation Board to celebrate the 50th
anniversary of the Cotswolds Area of Outstanding
Natural Beauty by Darien-Jones Publishing.

Designed and produced by Nicholas J Jones Graphics.

A CIP catalogue record for this book is available
from the British Library.

ISBN 978-1-902487-08-3

Printed using papers made from trees that have been
legally sourced from well-managed and credibly
certified forests.

Darien-Jones Publishing
PUBLISHERS OF MAPS & BOOKS

Tel: (01452) 812550 E-mail: sales@darien-jones.co.uk
www.darien-jones.co.uk

Cotswolds
Area of Outstanding
Natural Beauty

Front cover: Rolling Cotswold hills near Swainswick. Front flap: The Rollright Stones.
Back cover (top to bottom): The village of Castle Combe. A Cotswold dry stone wall. Frosty morning near Sherborne. Randwick Wap. Stanway House. The wool town of Painswick.

Below: The Cotswold escarpment and Cam Long Down viewed from Coaley Peak.

The
COTSWOLDS
Area of Outstanding Natural Beauty

NICK TURNER • SIÂN ELLIS • NICK DARIEN-JONES

CONTENTS

Left: The village of Snowshill.

Right: The quirky Compton Abdale crocodile fountain head.

INTRODUCTION

If you imagine a picture of rural England at its most idyllic, likely as not a vision of the Cotswolds springs to mind, of rolling hills, hidden valleys and pretty golden-stone cottages: scenes apparently untouched by time.

But every view tells a story and this book celebrates a much-loved landscape where each ridge and river, field and village reveals many tales of change. The very features that make the Cotswolds so special – its exhilarating western escarpment with panoramic vistas, the high wolds, ancient beech woods, wildflower grasslands, historic parks and gardens – have been formed and constantly transformed by nature, man or both together.

Framing everything, giving the Cotswolds its unique warmth, richness and visual harmony, is the famous local limestone: underfoot in the landscape and used in building the enchanting villages and market towns or farmland networks of dry stone walls. The limestone grasslands fed the sheep that brought huge wealth to the area in medieval times, bequeathing the fabulous legacy of 'wool churches' and manor houses so renowned to this day.

All this captivating splendour was officially recognised in 1966 when the Cotswolds was designated as an Area of Outstanding Natural Beauty (AONB), acknowledging it as one of our finest landscapes and a place to be looked after for future generations. At 790sq miles (2,038sq km), it is the largest of the family of 38 AONBs in England and Wales; achieving its 50th anniversary in 2016, it is also probably the best known and 23 million visitors a year come to enjoy it.

Meadows near Whittington look to the distant high wolds.

Left: Dunkirk Mill, Nailsworth.
Opposite page: The limestone village of Guiting Power.

For all the bustle of its honeypot towns, the AONB is still a place where it is possible to escape, to cycle, walk and stop and stare in peace and quiet. Then sunlight on fossils of a rocky outcrop or winter mist over a frosted river draws you back to a prehistoric Cotswolds of tropical seas or glacial meltwaters. Man has lived, worked and played here for more than 6,000 years, and you can read his life story in the landscape from Neolithic long barrows and Roman villas to cloth mills and canals, modern agriculture and recreational attractions.

The landscape – and local rootedness in it – truly influences everything, with an authenticity that both sticks to traditions and keeps evolving. You can taste it in mellow Single Gloucester cheese, admire it in Arts and Crafts architecture, read about it in the works of Laurie Lee. You might be baffled by it watching cheese rolling down Cooper's Hill or be blown away by it at The Big Feastival food-and-music extravaganza.

Like the seasons with their shape-shifting summer sun and shadows, autumn gold and winter snow, so the landscape is always changing. Yet in the essential truth of its beauty and unique character it is always the Cotswolds.

A Cotswold Lion sheep – the emblem of the Cotswolds Area of Outstanding Natural Beauty.

Right: The village of Horsley on a January day.

Below: Belas Knap Neolithic long barrow on Cleeve Hill dates from c. 3,000BC.

Below: The River Eye near Bourton-on-the-Water.

THE COTSWOLDS AT A GLANCE

The Cotswolds Area of Outstanding Natural Beauty lies upon the best-known section of an outcrop of Jurassic limestone running across England from Dorset to Yorkshire. This is most apparent in the central feature of the AONB, the Cotswold Hills, which crest in a dramatic escarpment on their western edges, also giving breathtaking vistas of the Vales of Evesham, Gloucester, Severn and Berkeley.

While historic villages snuggle beneath the scarp, internationally important beech woods and rare, flower-rich limestone grasslands swathe its face.

Then gently dipping away to the southeast, the landscape tumbles into the rolling wolds that give the Cotswolds its name, as well as deep-cut wooded river valleys. Open views of arable fields with woodland play nip and tuck with scenes of village and pasture.

Stretching from Somerset and Wiltshire up through Gloucestershire and Oxfordshire to Warwickshire and Worcestershire, the 790sq mile (2,038sq km) AONB is iconic rural England at its most seductive: dancing like an elegantly arched ballerina's foot between the World Heritage City of Bath to the south and World Heritage Site of Blenheim Palace to the east; between Shakespeare's Stratford-upon-Avon to the north and Regency Cheltenham to the west.

When it comes to getting around, Roman routes are still evident, including the arrow-straight Fosse Way (now the A433 and A429) that runs the whole length of the Cotswolds between Bath, Cirencester and Moreton-in-Marsh. Or let curiosity be your compass along typically winding lanes.

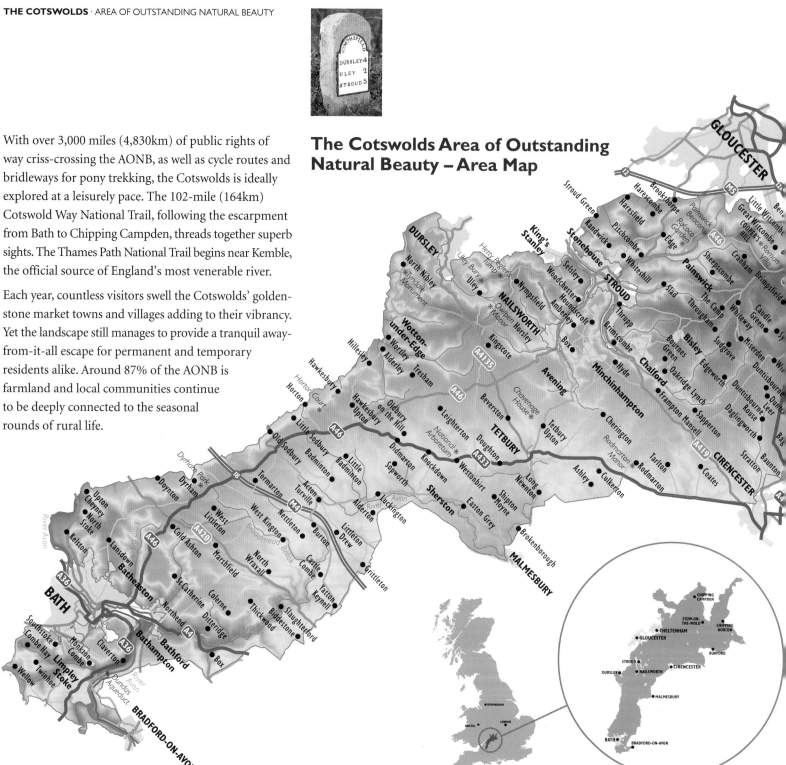

With over 3,000 miles (4,830km) of public rights of way criss-crossing the AONB, as well as cycle routes and bridleways for pony trekking, the Cotswolds is ideally explored at a leisurely pace. The 102-mile (164km) Cotswold Way National Trail, following the escarpment from Bath to Chipping Campden, threads together superb sights. The Thames Path National Trail begins near Kemble, the official source of England's most venerable river.

Each year, countless visitors swell the Cotswolds' golden-stone market towns and villages adding to their vibrancy. Yet the landscape still manages to provide a tranquil away-from-it-all escape for permanent and temporary residents alike. Around 87% of the AONB is farmland and local communities continue to be deeply connected to the seasonal rounds of rural life.

The Cotswolds Area of Outstanding Natural Beauty – Area Map

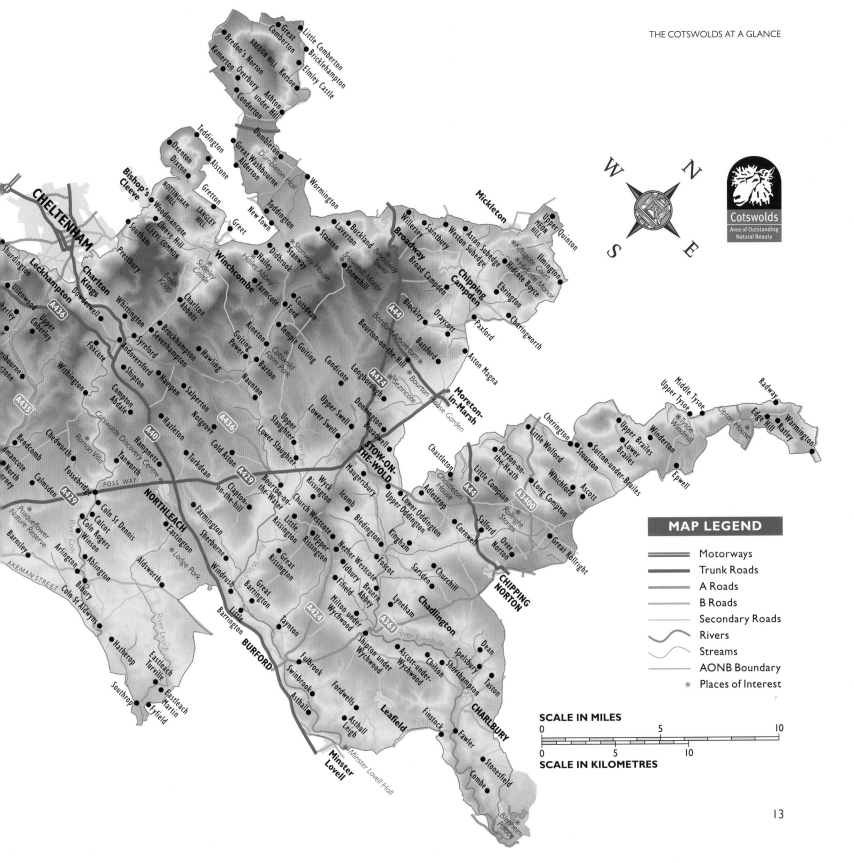

Cotswolds
Area of Outstanding
Natural Beauty

MAP LEGEND

Motorways
Trunk Roads
A Roads
B Roads
Secondary Roads
Rivers
Streams
AONB Boundary
* Places of Interest

SCALE IN MILES
0   5   10

SCALE IN KILOMETRES
0   5   10

13

Below: Beech trees and bluebells at Rough Park Nature Reserve, Cranham.

Left: An 18th-century windmill on Windmill Hill at Upper Tysoe.

Left: An ancient Cotswold stone footbridge reaches across the Sherborne Brook.

Below: Rolling hills near Broadway Tower.

CHAPTER ONE

The geology of the Cotswolds

The Cotswold escarpment looking towards Cheltenham from Cleeve Hill.

LIMESTONE

Left: Chastleton House near Moreton-in-Marsh.

Below: A Cotswold dry stone wall.

The story of the Cotswolds begins right beneath our feet with its rich geology, in particular the Jurassic limestone laid down 140–210 million years ago.

Typical Cotswold Jurassic rock is oolitic – meaning 'egg stone' – which describes the millions of particles that made it from the remains of exotic corals and shellfish that teemed in the warm, shallow seas covering the area at the time.

Limestone influences everything: from the way the rolling hills and valleys have been shaped, to the rare flora and fauna that flourish on them. It provided the right conditions for the wealthy medieval wool trade, and has built the dry stone walls, towns and villages whose organic unity with their landscape melts the heart.

While the honeyed limestone of the northern Cotswolds romantically hints at sunshine captured from its tropical origins, in reality variations in colour derive from the rock's iron oxide content: subtly shading into greys around Stroud, and pale creams around Bath.

Eminently workable, high-quality Cotswold stone has been used in many of the area's – and England's – grand buildings, such as wealthy 17th-century wool merchant's home Chastleton House near Moreton-in-Marsh and Blenheim Palace at Woodstock.

Quarrying, which dates from Roman times, continues on a modest scale to this day including at Naunton and Daglingworth – both among sites of copious fossil discoveries ranging from shellfish to dinosaur footprints. It's no coincidence that 'Father of English Geology' William Smith (1769–1839) hailed from Churchill in the Oxfordshire Cotswolds.

Right: A fossil of part of a lobster, Eryma guisei, found at Leckhampton Hill.

Below: Syreford Quarry.

THE ESCARPMENT

Left: 'The Twins' at the summit of Cleeve Hill.
Below: The Cotswold escarpment at Cleeve Hill, also known as Cleeve Cloud.

Stretching 52 miles (84km) in a near-continuous line northeast from Bath to Mickleton, the escarpment gives the western Cotswolds the most dramatic of sheer edges. A slumbering Jurassic giant, its gnarly rock face is laid bare here and there by the elements and quarrying, its summit gripped by narrow belts of trees silhouetted against the sky.

Vistas over the Severn and Avon Vales are breathtaking – and the giddying look back up is equally thrilling. At a puffing 1,083ft (330m), Cleeve Cloud is the loftiest point in the whole of the Cotswolds.

The epic movement of continents over the last 150–200 million years that pushed and tilted the Earth's crust to form the escarpment also created its distinctive backdrop falling away to the east: a classic 'scarp and dip' landscape.

Further activity gave the tale that the Devil made Meon Hill, at the tip of the Cotswold escarpment in Warwickshire, by throwing a clod of earth in a fit of anger. More prosaically, it's the result of millennia of erosion, which detached it from the scarp.

Along with similarly created outliers like the massive whaleback of Bredon Hill, Meon Hill became a noted landmark whose strategic value as a lookout made it a site of choice for an Iron Age hill fort.

A CROSS SECTION OF LECKHAMPTON HILL

1000 ft
Inferior Oolite
Midford Sands
Upper Lias Clay
Marlstone
500 ft
Lower Lias Clay
0 — Sea Level
0   1   2 Miles

"A man may do anything with Cotswold stone but eat it"
– An old Cotswold saying.

CHAPTER TWO

The Cotswold landscape and its unique habitats

Looking west from Nimlet, near Cold Ashton, over rolling hills so typical of the Cotswold landscape.

HIGH WOLDS AND ROLLING HILLS

Left: Rippling farmland and summer pasture in the Slad Valley.

Deep breath. Then feel your spirits swoop across the open wolds, away and up into endless skies, or down through rolling hills interlocking like fingers. Maybe a morning mist is unveiling a valley or late afternoon shadows are smudging trees over the fields.

The high wolds are simply exhilarating, sweeping in a broad, undulating plateau at the top and to the east of the escarpment, north of Stroud to Chipping Campden. Wraparound views unfurl a sense of windswept freedom, while further east and south the countryside melts into softer hills and valleys, more secret and intimate.

Our ancestors called the landscape as they saw it and 'wold', from an Old English word, referred to forest but later came to mean open rolling uplands.

Some say that the name 'Cotswolds' originally had to do with a wooded area held by a Saxon named Cot; the more populist interpretation is that it derives from 'sheep shelters' (cots) 'in rolling hills'. Be that as it may; the thin-soiled wolds have certainly suited grazing sheep.

Except for the hilltop town of Stow-on-the-Wold, the lofty plateau is only sparsely settled, edged here and there by commons. Remote. Quiet. Liberating.

Around and running away below, the landscape is a richly textured storybook of historical and seasonal change: large arable fields of green or brown stitched together by dry stone wall or hedge. Copses, shelterbelts, delves (shallow quarries), or strip lynchets terracing a hillside for cultivation. And those long, long views.

Left: Undulating hills, St Catherine's Valley north of Bath.

Below: The hilltop town of Stow-on-the-Wold.

Left: Downham Hill, near Cam.
Below: Sweeping views near Doynton.

Left: Dusk at Barrow Wake near Birdlip.

Left: Willows nod over the River Evenlode, near Bledington.

RIVERS, VALLEYS AND WATER MEADOWS

When morning frosts freeze the banks of the River Windrush at Sherborne, it's as if Earth memories are stirring, calling to mind primeval scenes when this beautiful valley was first created.

Through millennia numerous streams, eating into the porous Cotswold limestone, have fashioned river valleys in the landscape, while the melting of seasonal snowcaps following the Ice Ages gobbled broad and deep. Where meltwaters have vanished, the dry valleys are left or, as with the Windrush, you find 'misfit' valleys: the river now a narrow ghost of its post-glacial torrent.

Water is the pervasive mood music of the Cotswold landscape. Rivers like the Churn, Coln, Leach and Windrush rise on the scarp, follow the tilt of geology southeast, and along with the Evenlode join the Thames, which has its official source near Kemble. Others link with the River Severn or Avon, and you will find no more secretive river valleys than those incised around Bath and Stroud.

Quiet riverside wanderings can delight with glimpses of otters or kingfishers, or the plop of a water vole – its numbers on the rise again thanks to local conservation work. The clear waters of the aquifer-fed Coln, among others, are known for grayling and brown trout.

Water meadows, traditionally providing lush grazing and an 'early bite' for livestock, are also havens for flora and fauna, whether darting dragonflies over the restored 18th-century meadows at Sherborne or colourful marsh orchids, flag irises and marsh marigolds at Bibury.

Left: The River Avon at Bradford-on-Avon.

Below: Frosty morning on the Sherborne Brook, a tributary of the River Windrush.

ANCIENT BROADLEAF WOODLANDS

Left: Trees cling to the top of Haresfield Beacon.

The Cotswolds' ancient broadleaf woodlands, notably clinging to the western scarp and deep valley sides, are a heart-warming glory to behold, no more so than in autumn when the beech woods erupt into fiery oranges, gold and copper.

Following the Ice Age, most of the Cotswolds was shrouded by 'wildwood', before our hunter-gatherer ancestors and Neolithic farmers cleared ground for pasture and cultivation. Still, today, nearly 13% of the AONB is woodland, with almost one-sixth of it growing on ancient sites.

Beech trees recognised to be internationally important thrive on the limestone soils. At Lineover Wood on the scarp close to Dowdeswell one spectacular specimen is estimated to be over 600 years old, the girth of its trunk a portly 23 feet (7m), the third largest beech in England. Alongside oak and ash trees, Lineover is also blessed with many ancient large-leaved limes.

A little way southwest at Cranham, Buckholt Wood – the name is from the Saxon for 'beech wood' – casts a cathedral-like calm with its soaring boughs. Also look down to spot a few of the 780-plus species of fungi found here, their names like scarlet elfcup and amethyst deceiver so evocative of mystery.

Some species, including types of spiders, are dependent on ancient woodlands to survive and it's a joy to find lots of floral rarities, such as Solomon's seal and yellow star of Bethlehem at Colerne Park and Monk's Wood north of Bath.

> *"O the wild trees of home with their sounding dresses"*
> – 'The Wild Trees', Laurie Lee.

Left: Beech and oak leaves.

Below: Ancient beech trees on the Cotswold Way,
Lineover Wood, near Dowdeswell.

WILDFLOWER-RICH GRASSLANDS AND COMMONS

Left: Selsley Common.
Below: Wildflower meadows near Andoversford and Syreford.

There are few more iconic scenes of summer in the English countryside than wildflowers speckling grassland with their multicoloured jewels, certainly in the Cotswolds. Boasting over half of the UK's total Jurassic unimproved limestone grassland, much of it clustered along the escarpment, the AONB is a stronghold for orchids and other precious sights.

These wildflower-rich grasslands are the result of both nature and nurture: the underlying limestone combined with centuries of traditional animal grazing and farming 'unimproved' by the use of artificial fertilisers and chemicals. Across the UK such sites have been rapidly vanishing but in the Cotswolds some 400 remain.

Rare or unusual plants including the Cotswold pennycress flourish in the 'nutrient-poor' conditions, and the habitat is perfect for nationally rare butterflies like the chalkhill blue.

The UK's largest land snail also loves lime-rich soils: fattened on milk and herbs by the Romans to be eaten, *Helix pomatia* is now a protected species, living at Leckhampton Hill, Cooper's Hill and Chedworth Roman Villa.

Meanwhile, Swift's Hill (Elliott Nature Reserve) in the Slad Valley near Stroud, too steep to have been 'improved' for crop growing, stands in yellowy-green contrast to the bright green and brown of surrounding agricultural fields. Rare frog, bee and early purple orchids are among 130 species of wildflowers growing on the hill.

The commons of the escarpment – nearby Selsley, Minchinhampton and Rodborough, or Cleeve Common to the north – are equally wonderful wildflower sites.

Right: The Adonis blue butterfly – found on Rodborough Common.

Below: Swift's Hill Nature Reserve, near Stroud, where the unimproved grassland stands in contrast to the surrounding agricultural land.

Left: Pasqueflowers thrive in limestone grasslands.
Below: Farmland set aside for wildflowers.

Their shallow soils and exposed settings have been inhospitable to cultivation, but local people have exercised their rights to graze animals here since the earliest historical times. Alongside sensitive conservation work, sheep and cattle keep coarse grasses and scrub at bay.

On Cleeve Common, the Cotswolds' largest common at around 1,000 acres (400ha), a diversity of habitats are home to common lizards and grass snakes, yellowhammers and trilling skylarks. Rodborough Common is renowned for its butterflies, from colonies of iridescent Adonis blue and rare Duke of Burgundy to green hairstreak and marbled white.

Elsewhere, there's a spectacular late-spring treat in the dry valley of Barnsley Warren Site of Special Scientific Interest near Cirencester, when the purple petals of Britain's largest pasqueflower population burst forth.

Downland flora has also been quick to skip into former limestone quarries like Browne's Folly Nature Reserve east of Bath, while open rock faces at Cutsdean Quarry Nature Reserve provide the perfect spots for reptiles to bask in sunshine.

Duke of Burgundy.

"Wildflower grasslands are as important to our heritage as the works of Shakespeare"
– Plantlife.

Left to right: A marsh fritillary butterfly and butterfly orchid at Strawberry Hill Nature Reserve. A common lizard at Cutsdean Quarry Nature Reserve.

Below: Pasqueflower Nature Reserve, Barnsley Warren.

Left: A Cotswold dry stone wall with distinctive 'cock and hen' cope stones.

DRY STONE WALLS AND HEDGEROWS

Dry stone walls and hedgerows criss-cross the Cotswold landscape like character lines on a much-loved face, with more than 4,000 miles (6,440km) of such walls alone.

While local examples of dry stone walling date back 5,000 years to Neolithic long barrows, most that we see today originate from the enclosure of open fields and sheepwalks in the 18th and 19th centuries. Serving as boundaries and stock barriers – generally, walls on higher, thinner soils and ridge tops of the scarp, hedges on deeper soils – they imposed a new pattern on the countryside.

Much of the beauty of Cotswold field walls, typically built with the limestone closest to hand, lies in their differing hues and textures: using boulder-like stones near Bath, for example, or rough ragstone near Cheltenham. 'Cock and hen' cope stones alternating in height along the top of some walls give a characteristically Cotswold crown.

Dry stone walls also reveal fantastic habitat and busy wildlife corridors, as mosses and lichens add their patina to the stones, bees and wasps take up home, wrens and wheatears make nests. The UK's only population of the endangered *Lauria sempronii*, a small limestone-loving snail, lives in Cotswold stone walling.

Then in autumn the hedgerows come into their own as living larders, ripe with elderberries and sloes. Hedges at Radway Meadows Nature Reserve in the Warwickshire Cotswolds may be over 500 years old, a delicious picture of English elm, crab apple, willows and hawthorn, of summer-flowering dog rose and autumn's red hips.

Left: Peering over a wall to the village of Slad.
Below: Cotswold dry stone wall and hedgerows at Miserden.

CHAPTER THREE

Buildings in the landscape

The City of Bath viewed from Bath Skyline walk.

PREHISTORIC AND ROMAN REMAINS

Left: Belas Knap long barrow.
Below: Winter sunrise at the Rollright Stones.

In an instant the sight of a bulging Neolithic long barrow, the Rollright Stones, or the emphatic ridges of an Iron Age hill fort rekindles the world-view of those who walked the Cotswolds before us.

People have settled here for more than 6,000 years, interpreting and shaping the landscape, and with lots of local limestone suitable for building, large numbers of outstanding Neolithic (c. 4,000–2,500BC) and Bronze Age (c. 2,500–750BC) monuments have survived.

High in the hillsides, long barrow tombs like Belas Knap above Winchcombe and Hetty Pegler's Tump overlooking the Severn Vale speak even now of respect for the ancient dead and the symbolic power of dramatic scenery. Such barrows may even have served as territorial markers over valley communities below.

The ritual purpose of the Neolithic/Bronze Age Rollright Stones near Chipping Norton is much debated, the circle's alignment perhaps indicating an astronomical function; in folklore the circle and its adjacent stones are said to be a king, his men and three traitors petrified by a witch.

Later during the Iron Age, hill forts were built to make the most of commanding views from the escarpment, from the rippling ramparts of Meon Hill and Uley Bury to Little Solsbury Hill.

Then the Romans, arriving in the Cotswolds shortly after AD43, bequeathed roads like the Fosse Way and remarkable villas that highlighted their farming and commercial prosperity. Excavations of bath-house rooms, underfloor heating and superb mosaics at Chedworth Romano-British villa, Yanworth, suggest comforts surpassed only by the spa luxuries of *Aquae Sulis* (Bath) to the south.

Left: Great Witcombe Roman Villa, built around AD*250.*
Far left: Pilae from the underfloor heating, Chedworth Roman Villa.
Below: Uley Bury Iron Age hill fort.

HISTORIC HIGHLIGHTS

Left: Owlpen Manor near Uley derives its name from a local Saxon thegn.
Below: Sudeley Castle, Winchcombe.

The influence of the Anglo-Saxons, who filled the power vacuum left by Roman legions recalled to Rome in the early 5th century, is often overlooked. Yet they gave us 'Aengla Land' and the idea of Englishness, and they re-organised towns and countryside during the 800s and 900s to create a basis for much of the Cotswold landscape – quintessential England – we love today.

Among the best reminders of Anglo-Saxon culture, when Christianity flourished anew, is the tiny Saxon church of St Laurence at Bradford-on-Avon. Typically tall and narrow, with a rare richness of decoration, it is an extraordinary survivor and still used for worship.

Even Sudeley Castle, its walls glowing gold against green hills at Winchcombe, can trace estate connections back to the Saxon King Ethelred (the Unready) and his daughter Goda. Over 1,000 years since, history has layered on lively adventures here, and Sudeley is the only private castle in England to have a queen – Henry VIII's sixth wife, Katherine Parr – buried within its grounds.

Elsewhere historic monuments bear witness to battles that have further forged England's identity. Fifteenth-century Minster Lovell Hall, now a romantic riverside ruin, is reputedly haunted by Francis Lovell who, having fought on the wrong side in the Wars of the Roses, hid in a locked secret chamber, was forgotten and starved to death.

Battlefields tell tales of the English Civil War, at Edgehill (1642), Lansdown Hill (1643) and Stow-on-the-Wold (1646), the latter a decisive step towards the overthrow of King Charles I.

Far left: Ancient yews flank the doorway to 11th-century Stow-on-the-Wold church.
Left: Minster Lovell Hall.

COTSWOLD STONE TOWNS AND VILLAGES

Many a walker following the escarpment along the Cotswold Way has dropped down below Shenberrow Hill into Stanton and believed they are in heaven. Little-changed in 300 years, the quiet northern Cotswold village is an idyll of warm limestone houses, medieval church and 17th-century Mount Inn (with friendly ghost).

Stanton may be off the worn tourist track – you won't find shops here – but its buildings are typical of what makes Cotswold towns and villages so special. Built of locally quarried stone, they seem to spring organically from their surroundings and sit in mellow harmony with their landscape.

From the medieval era craftsmen-builders developed a distinctive Cotswold vernacular style: steep-pitched roofs with limestone slates increasing in size from ridge to eaves with the orderly beauty of fish scales; tall 'Jacobean' gables and tall, bold chimneys; mullioned windows and a rustic sense of balance and proportion to make the heart sing. A sprinkle of thatch adds a charming counterpoint.

Geology dictated where settlements spread, generally at the scarp's foot, in valley bottoms and on the gentler valley sides at spring lines, and many of today's towns and villages were already in existence by the time of the Domesday Book (1086–1087).

'Chipping', as in Chipping Norton, derives from Old English 'ceapen' meaning 'market' and points to the reason for the growth of many Cotswold towns. In the medieval heydays of wool production places like Burford, Stow-on-the-Wold, Northleach and Marshfield throbbed with trade, and when wool fortunes waned numerous towns bustled anew as staging posts on important stagecoach routes.

Left: The wool town of Northleach viewed from the church tower.

Above: The market cross in Stow-on-the-Wold square.

Below: Duntisbourne Leer.

Left: Tetbury's 17th-century Market House.
Below: 'Heavenly' Stanton in high summer.

Left: Hampnett village.
Below left: Chipping Campden Market Hall.

In the economic doldrums between times 'Poverty the Preserver' ensured that the vernacular architecture of such towns wasn't swept away by invasive new fashions, but was left to be loved by later generations and become a magnet for tourism.

The 17th-century pillared market halls at Chipping Campden and Tetbury, still hosting markets, remain wonderful town centrepieces. Former coaching inns at Burford and along Broadway's chestnut-lined High Street still refresh visitors. All joined by the modern temptations of antiques shops, art galleries and diverse other independent retailers.

Which is the most attractive Cotswold town or village? It's an impossible but often asked question. Bourton-on-the-Water with its picturesque five bridges over the River Windrush is certainly among the most visited and even its model village, an exquisitely accurate replica of Bourton, is protected under Grade II listing.

Some cite Upper and Lower Slaughter as prettiest of the pretty, their cottages beside the River Eye the romantic epitome of Cotswold living, though the curious Slaughter name – from Old English 'slohtre' meaning 'muddy place' – suggests this wasn't always 'des res'.

Alternatively, author Henry James plumped for Broadway and surrounds, "the perfection of the old English rural tradition". Most famously Victorian Arts and Crafts pioneer William Morris declared Bibury "the most beautiful village in England". Not for nothing do the 17th-century weavers' cottages jostling along Arlington Row appear as an iconic image of England inside modern UK passports.

Attractively diverse architectural styles in Burford.

Left: Riverside Coln Rogers.

*Below: Arlington Row, near Bibury –
iconic England – in winter.*

Left and below left: Miserden village scenes.
Bottom left: Upper Slaughter.

Left: Guiting Power church.
Below: Yanworth, prettily tucked amid fields and trees.

COUNTRY HOUSES AND ESTATES

Left: Lodge Park, Sherborne.
Below: Chavenage House near Tetbury.
Bottom: Blenheim Palace, Woodstock.

What more beguiling marriage of fashionable taste and workaday toil than a handsome country house in a well-tended estate?

Numerous local mansions arose following Henry VIII's Dissolution of the Monasteries in the 16th century, when the king's confiscation of monastic property triggered a dramatic change over large swathes of countryside. Suddenly, those with wealth or title had the opportunity to acquire new land on which to build homes befitting their status, leading in time to glories like Chavenage House and Stanway House.

Chavenage, near Tetbury, is a classic Elizabethan manor with two wings and porch, now home to the Lowsley-Williams family and a favourite location among period filmmakers.

Owned by Tewkesbury Abbey and then for the last 500 years by the Tracy family and their descendants, the Earls of Wemyss, Stanway boasts the most beautiful Jacobean gabled manor house and a magnificent gatehouse. The present Earl maintains the estate, including five villages, farms, parkland and woodland, to preserve its traditional character while also innovating – the world's tallest gravity-fed fountain is a must-see for visitors.

Among estates of more recent vintage, Blenheim Palace at Woodstock dazzles as the 18th-century baroque masterpiece created to celebrate the victories of the 1st Duke of Marlborough in the War of the Spanish Succession. Hand in hand with tradition the vital activities of a modern working estate continue here too, from sensitive farming and a new eco-business office development to production of mineral water sourced from the limestone aquifer deep beneath the Cotswolds.

*Left: The magnificent gatehouse
of Stanway House.*

Below: Dumbleton Hall.

51

HISTORIC PARKS AND GARDENS

Left: A quiet corner at Hidcote.
Below: Bourton House Garden.
Bottom: Kiftsgate Court Lower Garden.

Intoxicating summer scents from roses, a water garden striking a cool contrast in black, white and green: these are just two of the thrilling surprises at Kiftsgate Court Gardens on the escarpment edge near Chipping Campden. Created in modern times by three generations of green-fingered women, Kiftsgate is among the latest in a long succession of exceptional local gardens, inspired by and embellishing their surroundings. Together they give an extraordinary record of changing horticultural fashions.

Stroll back 400 years at Chastleton House, near Moreton-in-Marsh, to a garden divided into Jacobean-style compartments. Explore the rare, restored 18th-century pleasure park of flamboyant follies and water features at Painswick Rococo Garden.

The 18th century was also the era of magnificent parks and landscape gardening – witness Blenheim Palace, Prior Park Landscape Garden below the Bath Skyline walk and Cirencester Park with its avenues and rides. Sezincote, Bourton-on-the-Hill, then comes as a shock: a Mogul Indian palace with exotic gardens right in the Cotswolds.

Victorian plant hunters had an eye to the unusual, too, and Westonbirt, The National Arboretum, and Batsford Arboretum are particularly splendid for autumn colour. Gardens at Upton House near Banbury revive a 1930s leisure haven, and Arts and Crafts outdoor 'rooms' at Hidcote near Chipping Campden have influenced gardeners around the world.

Taking a lead into the future, Prince Charles works with nature, championing organic and sustainable principles, in the gardens at his Highgrove home near Tetbury. Here he has created interlinked areas that 'feed the soul', including an iconic Wild Flower Meadow.

*Left and below: The Water Garden
and roses at Kiftsgate Court.*

WOOL HERITAGE

Wealth generated by the 'Golden Fleece' of Cotswold sheep in the late medieval boom time of the wool trade has left a quite unrivalled legacy of market town architecture, manors, merchants' houses and 'wool churches' across the region.

The Romans probably introduced the forerunner of Cotswold sheep, although like the populist derivation of 'Cots' (sheep shelters) 'wolds' (in rolling hills), the specific origins of the breed are elusive. What is certain is that local thin-soiled limestone slopes favoured sheep grazing. The 'Cotswold Lion' thrived, in demand for its long, curly, lustrous wool for spinning into worsted yarn.

Local Jurassic limestone also provided fuller's earth, used to remove grease from fleeces, and with plenty of clear streams for washing, the Cotswolds had a natural advantage in the wool business from the outset.

Monasteries and abbeys like Hailes and Cirencester ran huge early flocks of sheep, and as wool exports developed, particularly to the Low Countries, landowners and merchants grew rich on trade. Perhaps 500,000 sheep roamed the Cotswolds in their medieval heyday, while in the 18th century it's said 20,000 were sold on a good day in Stow-on-the-Wold – you can still squeeze through 'tures' (narrow alleyways) built to filter animals into the square.

With an eye to investment in the afterlife as well as the earthly comforts of fine homes, wealthy merchants endowed schools, almshouses and, the enduring symbol of the times, churches.

St James' Church, Chipping Campden, its West Tower soaring above the town, is a stunning example. Memorials inside include a 15th-century brass commemorating

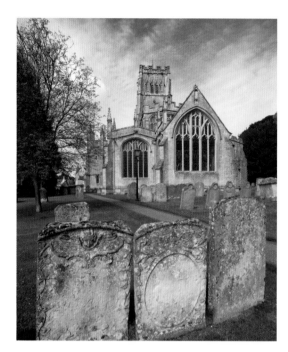

Left: The Church of St Peter & St Paul, Northleach.

Below right: Chipping Campden.

Wool trade motifs in memorial windows in the chapel of the Perry and Dawes Almshouses, Wotton-under-Edge.

Right: Sheep Street sign in Chipping Campden.

"I thank God and ever shall – It is the Sheepe hath payed for all"
– Inscribed in the house of a Merchant of the Staple.

Left: Wool merchants depicted in stained glass and memorial brasses in Northleach church.

William Grevel, "flower of the wool merchants of all England". His impressive home, Grevel House, resplendent with carved windows, gargoyles and a sundial, is along the High Street, opposite the 14th-century Woolstaplers' Hall where fleeces were sold.

St Peter & St Paul, Northleach, rebuilt in the 15th century, is full of memorial brasses depicting its benefactors, sheep and woolpacks at their feet. St John Baptist at Cirencester, St Mary's at Chipping Norton and Burford Church are also architecturally outstanding, while St Mary's at Painswick is remarkable for its ornate churchyard memorials to 17th/18th-century clothiers and merchants.

As woollen cloth manufacture took over from raw fleece exports, locations like Painswick with fast-flowing streams to power fulling mills prospered. Around the Cotswolds the evolution of weaving and cloth making is etched into streetscapes, from weavers' cottages at Castle Combe and on the hillside at Bradford-on-Avon, to the mills, terraces and clothiers' townhouses shoehorned into the Stroud Valleys.

By the 1700s there were some 170 active mill sites around Stroud and trade was truly international. Hardwearing broadcloth dyed in Stroud Scarlet or Uley Blue became much used in Army and Royal Navy uniforms, while West of England cloth became *de rigueur* for suits.

Eventually competition, including from steam-powered mills in northern towns, sent the local cloth industry into decline in the 19th century. Yet many mills remain, transformed into heritage attractions, offices or homes. Traditions continue at Stroud's Lodgemore Mill, today making cloth for billiard sports and tennis ball coverings, and also at Cotswold Woollen Weavers at Filkins.

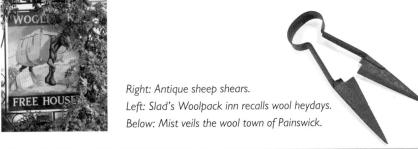

Below left: Bliss Tweed Mill at Chipping Norton, now luxury apartments.

Right: Antique sheep shears.

Left: Slad's Woolpack inn recalls wool heydays.

Below: Mist veils the wool town of Painswick.

57

ALONG THE CANALS

Left: Sapperton Tunnel on the Thames & Severn Canal.

Canal building in the 18th century promised to put the Cotswolds in the fast lane of commerce as new waterways provided an easier, more cost-effective method of transporting goods than unreliable roads through rolling hills and secluded valleys.

The Stroudwater Navigation (1779) and Thames & Severn Canal (1789), known collectively as the Cotswold Canals, made the all-important link between England's two great rivers, the Severn at Framilode and the Thames at Lechlade. Climbing from the Severn Plain via locks, the waterway took cargoes through the Golden Valley and Sapperton Tunnel beneath the Cotswold Hills, at 2.17 miles (3.5km) once the world's longest transportation tunnel.

Bringing coal to steam-powered textile mills around Stroud, the waterways were a great success – until overtaken by the arrival of the railways from the mid-19th century. Turn and turn about, ongoing restoration is now transforming fortunes again as the canals become escape routes from frenetic 21st-century life, gentler-paced leisure highways for boat trips, towpath walking and cycling.

To the south, Bradford-on-Avon was the busiest wharf on the Kennet & Avon Canal (completed 1810) that carried coal from the Somerset coalfields as well as bulky goods like cheeses.

Restored and re-opened in 1990, 'the K&A' is among the most well-loved waterways for narrowboating. The eight-mile (13km) towpath saunter from Bradford to Bath includes especially attractive scenery as well as canal engineer John Rennie's finest architectural achievement at Dundas Aqueduct. If you are lucky you might spot a kingfisher too, alongside ducks, heron and other wildlife.

Left: Chalford Roundhouse, once home to a lengthman who looked after a stretch of the Thames & Severn Canal.

Bottom: The Kennet & Avon Canal near Bath.

CHAPTER FOUR

Cultural heritage

A Roman re-enactment event at Chedworth Roman Villa.

Left: The stickler referees shin kicking on Dover's Hill.

Below: Cheese rolling, Cooper's Hill.

CURIOUS CUSTOMS

Where there's a steep hill, what is more natural than to chase a 7–8lb (3.2–3.6kg) Double Gloucester cheese down it?

The challenge certainly thrills the crowds at Cooper's Hill on the escarpment at Brockworth, though no one is entirely sure of the roots of this May custom, whether it began in Roman times, was a rite of passage for local lads, or derives from some other bright idea.

The Cotswold Olimpicks, drawing spectators to the natural amphitheatre of Dover's Hill above Chipping Campden in late spring, has a firmer recorded origin dating from 1612 when lawyer Robert Dover promoted the games to encourage manly sports "for the harmless mirthe and jollitie of the neighbourhood". Strangely, disciplines like shin kicking (the aim is to unbalance opponents and throw them) didn't catch on in the modern Olympics that the games helped to inspire.

Eccentric, colourful traditions are the social glue of rural life and the Cotswolds excels in them: marking the seasonal round from the Ascension Day custom of Bisley Well Dressing, to Painswick Feast Day 'clypping' ceremony in September when St Mary's Church is encircled in dance and song.

Spring's Randwick Wap combines pagan and Christian elements with the dunking of the Mayor at the Mayor's Pool. The Marshfield Mummers, performing on Boxing Day, invoke fertility rituals and medieval drama. Woollen heritage is upheld – literally – at Tetbury Woolsack Races on Gumstool Hill; once the way for muscular young drovers to impress local women, today it's – allegedly – fun.

"Let love and friendship still agree – To hold the Banns of Amity"
– The chorus from the Mayor's song, sung at Randwick Wap (left).

THE LITERARY LANDSCAPE

Left: William Shakespeare's statue in Stratford-upon-Avon.
Below: The Laurie Lee Wildlife Way at Slad features poetry by the local-born author on each waymarker.

No one has evoked the lyrical beauty of the Cotswold landscape more passionately than Laurie Lee in *Cider with Rosie*, his bestselling, bittersweet memoir of childhood and change in Slad post-World War One: the valley with its "secret origins, having been gouged from the escarpment by the melting ice-caps"; light on the slopes, with cattle "brilliant as china, treading their echoing shapes"; beech trees sunlit "as though clogged with wild wet honey".

To this day the landmarks that gave Lee's imagination flight – The Woolpack inn, church, hills – are still to be enjoyed, and poetry posts inscribed with his verse can be followed on the Laurie Lee Wildlife Way through trees "with their sounding dresses".

Many authors before and since have made their connections with the countryside, A E Housman writing of love and loss in 'Bredon Hill'; WWI poet Ivor Gurney imagining peace away from trench warfare in "soft winter's mornings of kind innocence" on Cooper's Hill in 'That Centre of Old'. J R R Tolkien based Middle Earth's The Prancing Pony on The Bell Inn, Moreton-in-Marsh, and Jilly Cooper's blockbuster equine romps would be incomplete without their Cotswoldian backdrops.

It's even claimed that William Shakespeare spent his 'lost years' (when he vanished from Stratford after being caught poaching) school teaching in Dursley – accounting for his knowledge of Gloucestershire's "high wild hills and rough uneven ways" in *Richard II*. Meanwhile William Tyndale, who opened up the Scriptures to the common man in his 'ploughboy's Bible', has a worthy monument at North Nibley.

Fact and fiction are celebrated in all forms at lively literary festivals from Cheltenham to Chipping Norton.

Left: The Tyndale Monument, North Nibley.

Below: Bredon Hill, where Housman mused on love, is crowned by an Iron Age hill fort.

WILLIAM MORRIS AND THE ARTS AND CRAFTS MOVEMENT

Left: Relief carving of William Morris near Kelmscott Manor.
Below: Morris & Co Arts and Crafts stained glass at Selsley church.

It remains a wonderful irony that the Cotswolds' decline following its wool heydays proved the seed for its revival. A down-at-heel 19th-century backwater largely untouched by the Industrial Revolution, the region enchanted the pioneers of the Arts and Crafts movement (1880s–c.1940) who 'rediscovered' its rural appeal and vernacular limestone architecture.

Here, far from what they saw as the dehumanising crush of industry, traditional handcrafts prevailed with honest simplicity and respect for materials fit for purpose. There was nature to inspire, fresh air and an authentic way of life, all suiting the ideal for a place to practise art and craft as forces for good – aesthetic, moral and social.

William Morris led the influx, finding a homely "heaven on earth" – and source material in river and garden for famous textile designs – at Kelmscott Manor, also using Broadway Tower as a studio. Morris & Co stained glass is a glory of All Saints Church at Selsley, while clumsy restoration work at Burford Church spurred Morris to co-found The Society for the Protection of Ancient Buildings in 1877.

Arts and Crafts groups sprang up in Broadway, Chipping Campden, Sapperton, and the movement's inheritors left legacies across the Cotswolds: Rodmarton Manor – "The English Arts and Crafts Movement at its best" – built and furnished by Ernest Barnsley and fellow craftsmen; Detmar Blow's Hilles House rising like a natural outcrop of the escarpment near Painswick.

Momentum continues apace in the 21st century, whether through Gloucestershire Guild of Craftsmen or SITselect (formerly Stroud International Textiles).

Right: Kelmscott Manor – home of William Morris.
Below: Hilles House, Arts and Crafts period house designed by Detmar Blow, a pupil of John Ruskin.

"It was in those days ... IMPOSSIBLE for an artisan to produce less than his best"
– Edward Barnsley.

ARTS AND ARTISTS

"With the exception of love, there is perhaps nothing else by which people of all kinds are more united than by their pleasure in a good view."

So wrote Kenneth Clark in *Landscape into Art* (1949) and his comment could easily apply to any number of vistas from the escarpment, Bath Skyline walk or Ilmington Downs as sun, shadows and seasons paint their changing colours and moods.

Artists drawn to these dramatic landscapes are following in rich traditions. In the later 19th century, just as Arts and Crafts folk discovered the Cotswolds, the vogue for artists' colonies in picturesque corners of Britain saw the arrival in Broadway of Francis Davis Millet, John Singer Sargent and other noted painters, as well as writers like Henry James. It's still a hotspot for artists and galleries as well as home to the biennial Broadway Arts Festival.

From Winchcombe Festival of Music and Arts to Quenington's biennial Fresh Air sculpture shows contemporary talents find a stage to explore, express and excite creativity. Art Couture Painswick parades extraordinary wearable art among the iconic yew trees of the church every other year and showcases unique items in its gallery.

It's said that bohemian Stroud has more artists per capita than almost anywhere in Britain, and at Chalford over the past 30 years Pangolin Editions has been casting work for the country's foremost sculptors, the late Lynn Chadwick to Damien Hirst. Famous for his animals preserved in formaldehyde, spin paintings and spot paintings, Hirst also has studios in the Cotswolds.

Cotswold landscape painter Ian Shearman paints on Selsley Common.

MUSIC, THEATRE AND ENTERTAINMENT

Left: Street musicians at 'Chippy Jazz', Chipping Norton.

'Solsbury Hill', Peter Gabriel's debut single after leaving rock band Genesis, is a classic of letting go and looking to new experiences ("Climbing up on Solsbury Hill … Wind was blowing, time stood still"). And perhaps it's not surprising that the evocative flat-topped landmark, site of an Iron Age hill fort, should conspire with the elements to provide Gabriel with his spiritual motif.

When it comes to exploring new territory the performing arts scene around the Cotswolds is nothing if not diverse. *The Planets* composer Gustav Holst, born in Cheltenham, loved walking and practised his trombone in the hills, predilections commemorated by the 35-mile (56km) Gustav Holst Way from Cranham to Wyck Rissington where he had his first job as an organist, 1892–1893.

Quite a contrast, then, are the sounds that came out of Chipping Norton Recording Studios from the 1970s to 1990s from the likes of Gerry Rafferty, Status Quo, Jeff Beck, Alison Moyet and Radiohead. To this day Real World Studios in Box produces some of the best world music.

Many a pop star has settled in the Cotswolds and al fresco festivals, from 2000trees at Withington to The Big Feastival on Blur bassist Alex James' Kingham farm, crank up the summer volume.

Longborough Festival Opera performances take place in a bijou converted cattle shed, the Cotswold Arcadians bring open-air Shakespeare to Hatherop Castle, and Giffords Circus conjures up the pure childhood magic of a village green circus.

Gustav Holst statue in Cheltenham.

Left: The Cotswold Arcadians perform Shakespeare's Richard III at Hatherop Castle School.

Below: Cotswolds-based Giffords Circus on Minchinhampton Common.

TASTES AND TOASTS

Left: Double Gloucester cheese in maturation.
Below: Harvesting apples at Day's Cottage heritage orchard, Brookthorpe.

Wild garlic soup wafting aromas of woods in spring; fresh fish from Bibury Trout Farm, succulent lamb or sizzling Gloucestershire Old Spot pork. Summer strawberries gleaming in farmhouse cream, autumn ciders, herb-marinated Cotswold venison pie. Such irresistible treats roll around the mouth with the seasons.

Local producers have truly embraced the contemporary food revolution for all that is artisanal, sustainable and gloriously gourmet. But then farming has stocked the landscape larder for centuries and provides rich pickings for today's delis, farm shops, pubs, restaurants and foodie festivals. Modern farmers' markets, from Bath (the UK's first) to 'Covent Garden of the Cotswolds' Stroud, channel the spirit of medieval markets and fairs passed down in local DNA.

Cheeses are a highlight including mellow Single Gloucester boasting Protected Designation of Origin status, or how about a creamy, organic Brie from Simon Weaver whose cows graze meadows beside the River Dikler. The region also oozes with juices and ciders; Day's Cottage orchards at Brookthorpe grow over 200 varieties of apples, 105 of them indigenous to Gloucestershire.

Picturesque Donnington Brewery, drawing water used in its beers from the spring beside the millpond, is the only brewery in the world still powered by the same Victorian waterwheel, while Hook Norton Brewery is the country's finest example of a Victorian tower brewery: Cotswold water from the wells beneath it is a key ingredient in beers here, too, and – a toast to tradition – shire horses are still used to make deliveries to local pubs.

"Never to be forgotten, that first long secret drink of golden fire"
– From *Cider with Rosie*, Laurie Lee.

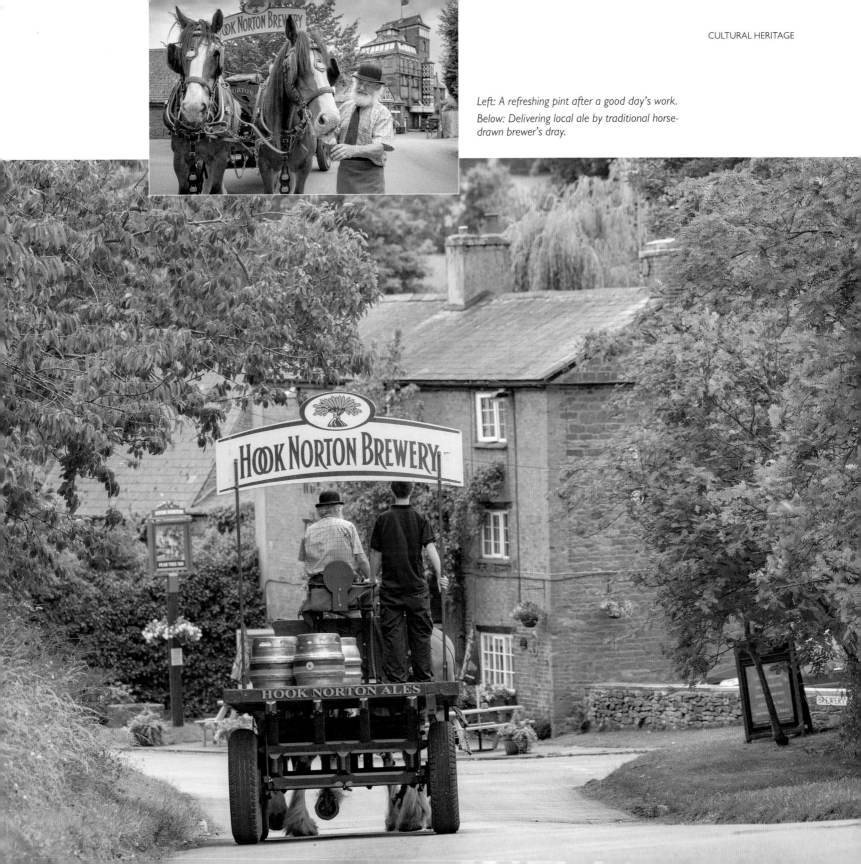

Left: A refreshing pint after a good day's work.
Below: Delivering local ale by traditional horse-drawn brewer's dray.

Left: Polo action at Beaufort Polo Club near Tetbury.

SPORTING LIFE

The echoing thwack of leather on willow and the occasional "howzat!" are synonymous with English country life in high summer. Add an attractive backdrop – the wooded hills above Dumbleton's club ground are just one example – and the scene is perfect for village cricket.

Think of a rural sporting pursuit – hunting, shooting, fishing – and it takes place around the AONB. Equine activity looms large with plenty of wide, open space for racehorse stables and gallops under the watchful eyes of champion trainers like Jonjo O'Neill at Guiting Power and Nigel Twiston-Davies at Naunton. Handy for Bath, Cheltenham and Stratford-upon-Avon racecourses!

More sheltered, estates and parks have made the area a major centre for polo, with The Beaufort Polo Club and Cirencester Park Polo Club where you might see The Duke of Cambridge or Prince Harry take the field. Badminton Horse Trials and the Festival of British Eventing at The Princess Royal's Gatcombe Park draw thousands of spectators.

Or get away from it all with a 'high tee': golf courses at Broadway, Cleeve Common and Cotswold Edge Golf Club enjoy the most breathtaking views.

Back down to earth, Bourton-on-the-Water River Football in August has been making a splash in the River Windrush since 1880. And if locals aren't putting a twist on conventional sport, they have been trailblazing: badminton was invented at Badminton House in 1863, and in 1866 the field rules of croquet were codified at Chastleton House, Moreton-in-Marsh. Where better to pick up a summer mallet?

Left: Football in the River Windrush at Bourton-on-the-Water.

Below: Cricket in Dumbleton's idyllic setting.

"I do love cricket – it's so very English"
– French actress Sarah Bernhardt, on seeing a game of football.

CHAPTER FIVE

Enjoying the countryside

Westonbirt, The National Arboretum, where walkers can enjoy spectacular autumn colours.

THE COTSWOLD WAY AND WALKING

Walkers on the Winchcombe Way (left) and on the Cotswold Way at Painswick (below).

An ultra-marathon runner in a hurry has previously completed the 102-mile (164km) Cotswold Way National Trail in well under 20 hours. Most people, quite rightly, ramble the route at a more leisurely pace, savouring the kaleidoscopic scenery along the escarpment from Bath to Chipping Campden: beech woods and meadows, follies and battlefields, hazy hills on far horizons and swooping lanes into comely villages – the Cotswold Way has it all.

The trail's beauty lies in its diversity, linking landmarks from Dyrham Park to the Tyndale Monument, Hailes Abbey and Stanway Estate, with lots of circular 'taster' walks like The Leckhampton Loop or Old Sodbury to the hill fort and church. Geocaching exercises the brain cells, too, while teashops and pubs en route offer ample opportunities to luxuriate in the afterglow of a brisk step.

The Cotswold Way is just the start. More than 20 long-distance routes and 3,000 miles (4,830km) of public rights of way weave through the AONB. Today: head through hills past 'lost' medieval villages on the Windrush Way, tomorrow, around leafy Wychwood. 'Walkers are Welcome' towns from Charlbury to Corsham and events like Winchcombe Cotswolds Walking Festival (late spring) add to the area's reputation as a hiker's heaven.

Always out and about, Cotswold Voluntary Wardens keep paths in good order and lead sociable guided walks. There are 'miles without stiles' and 'walks on wheels' (children's buggies to wheelchairs); and really no excuse to resist the lure of a waymarker pointing to escape. At the pace Nature intended.

Left: Cotswold Voluntary Wardens help maintain the walking trails.
Below: The Cotswold Way near Coaley Peak.

CYCLING

Left: Cycling on a summer day.
Below: A cross-country cyclist tackles Juniper Hill, near Painswick.

Whether relaxing or racy, the rhythmic pump of pedal and wheel does wonders for body and soul, and cycling, like walking, is a top leisure activity around the AONB. Local lanes – some originally designed for sheep droving – are ideal for a spin, and an exceptional abundance of good byways and bridleways beckon to off-road adventure.

Crossing the hills from east to west, from Oxford then up to Worcester, the scenic 77-mile (124km) Cotswold Line Cycle Route (National Cycle Network route 442) is a picturesque introduction via quiet lanes, tracks and towns like Moreton-in-Marsh – with a railway station every ten miles for lazy returns.

Easyriders love the Cotswolds' gentler southern slopes, adrenaline junkies the sharper escarpments of the north with the chance to hit big hills around Broadway and Weston Subedge. Pulse-racing, muscle-bracing off-road challenges roll around the Vale of Feldon, over the Ironstone Hills and around Brailes Hill. There are whirls through the high wold, challenges around Chedworth and exhilarating mountain biking.

Warm-downs and 'flat-out' fun include the attractive Kennet & Avon Cycle Route along the towpath from Bath to Bradford-on-Avon, part of Britain's most popular long-distance waterside cycle route; look out for the stunning aqueducts at Dundas and Avoncliff.

Left: Mountain bikers enjoy an adventure.

Below: The Tour de France cycling race when it passed through Winchcombe on the British stage.

RECREATION

Horse riding and hot air ballooning are popular recreational activities in the Cotswolds.

After dragon-like puffs and roars, and the ascent into the sky, there's just the whispering creak of the basket drifting through an airy dawn or late afternoon stillness. Below, the secrets of woodlands and fields, villages and lanes unfurl. Hot air ballooning – companies launch from sites including Stroud and Bourton-on-the-Water – is a magical way to admire patterns of farmland, hills and settlements in 360-degree splendour.

Brave hearts also enjoy excellent heights for paragliding and hang gliding over the Stroud Commons, stepping with heart-stopping daring into thin air to soar over the most fantastic bird's eye views. Gliding clubs at Nympsfield and Aston Down Airfield make the most of the Cotswold Edge and local ridges to gain lift, as well as using the abundant thermals rising from the well-drained Cotswold limestone.

Those who prefer terra firma can trot the landscape by horseback along bridleways and byways with wide-ranging appeal. The long-distance Sabrina Way runs from the Claude Duval Bridleroute at Great Barrington and hiring hooves at local riding centres to join group hacks to explore the countryside is a popular pastime.

Even more down to earth, Morris dancing, ubiquitous around the AONB, requires just two feet (and possibly hankies and sticks). Cotswold Morris is perhaps the best-known variety of the tradition, while Chipping Campden Morris is among the most unusual with its unique 'bicycle' step.

> *"Today is a day for the country ... Every hour indoors is an hour wasted"*
> – Ernest Gimson.

Left: Morris dancers at Eastleach Turville.
Below: Paragliding at Coaley Peak.

CHAPTER SIX

Working and caring for the Cotswolds

*Adam Henson, farmer and broadcaster, at Bemborough Farm,
near Kineton.*

FARMING

Left: A Belted Galloway cow grazes on Rodborough Common.

Farming, more than any other human activity, has shaped the Cotswold countryside and continues to do so today with some 87% of the AONB classed as agricultural. All those appealingly 'timeless' scenes and reassuring seasonal cycles evoke the deepest connections between man and earth: patchwork fields, sowing, harvesting, lambing and shearing, country shows, plough matches and wassailing.

In truth, the farming landscape has constantly changed within the seasonal round, from Neolithic woodland clearances to Roman wool and corn production, and the medieval heyday of the Cotswold Lion sheep roaming the limestone grasslands.

Subsistence strip farming and the earthen corrugations of medieval ridge-and-furrow gave way to 18th/19th-century enclosures of open field and downland. Hi-tech machinery overtook the wooden wagons now on show at the Lloyd Baker Rural Life Collection (the Cotswolds Discovery Centre, Northleach).

Today, mixed and arable farming have spread as once-extensive flocks of sheep have reduced, and around two-thirds of local land is currently under agri-environment schemes that benefit wildlife and biodiversity.

The Cotswolds boasts some wonderful farm animal breeds like the Khaki Campbell duck from Uley; Burford Brown, 'Britain's favourite hen', laying eggs with deep-brown shells; and the Cotswold Legbar hen that produces eggs with lovely pastel-blue shells.

But above all, the region is most famous for the iconic longwool Cotswold sheep, its shaggy forelock traditionally left after shearing to enable potential buyers to feel the quality of its fleece; the fatty, flavoursome Gloucestershire

Left: Gloucestershire Old Spot pigs.

Below: After the harvest – late summer near Hawkesbury Upton.

Left: Horses graze above Naunton.
Below: Simon Cooper, flax grower, Minchinhampton.

Old Spot pig, an 'orchard pig' whose distinctive spots were said to have been caused by falling apples; and mahogany-and-white Gloucester cattle, originally kept for draught work, meat and milk – used in Double and Single Gloucester cheeses.

For a while traditional breeds like these three lost favour as tastes changed and high-production farming went in for specialist single-purpose stock, but now they have their fans again, not least due to the revival of interest in local produce.

They – and other old, multi-purpose and rare native breeds – are celebrated at Adam Henson's Cotswold Farm Park at Kineton, which highlights the importance of maintaining diversity in the farm animal gene pool in order to meet potential future needs. Opened in 1971 by the late Joe Henson – also founder chairman of the Rare Breeds Survival Trust (RBST) – the park, part of a much larger farming business, flourishes under Joe's TV broadcasting son and farmer, Adam.

Nor is Adam the Cotswolds' only famous farmer. Prince Charles, patron of the RBST, has pioneered organic farming on the Duchy Home Farm near Tetbury since the 1980s and Princess Anne, patron of the Gloucestershire Old Spots Pig Breeders' Club, farms Old Spots among other animals on her Gatcombe Estate.

Meanwhile, right across the AONB countless farmers whose names will never be in the limelight quietly continue their custodianship of the countryside: balancing modern demands for ever more food production with environmental and climate challenges, while sustaining the spirit and beauty of the Cotswold landscape.

Bottom left: Ploughed field near Taddington.

Left: Steve Parkes, Cotswold Lion sheep breeder, Bourton-on-the-Water.

Below: Farmland near Postlip.

CRAFTSPEOPLE AND OLD TRADES

Left: Autumn hedgelaying at Fosse Cross.
Below: Thatcher Dan Quartermain works on a cottage roof at Wroxton.

It should be no surprise that Smith is England's most common name and there are plenty of Weavers, Potters, Thatchers, Turners and Wrights. Once, every town and village had its complement of craftspeople and tradesmen to service needs ranging from making farm implements and domestic wares to building.

In the Cotswolds, artisanal traditions have left a particularly strong mark, whether in dry stone walling, stone slate roofing or thatching, features that attracted Arts and Crafts pioneers to the area. While changes in land management practices have reduced the call for many rural hand skills, local crafts continue to evolve and adapt as creative forces, finding new expression while still underpinning the vernacular character of the AONB.

Dry stone wallers, for example, employ a more modern, regular-looking 'coursed' approach to building alongside the traditional farm labourers' 'random' technique. Blacksmith Richard Williams undertakes agricultural repairs at the family forge near Tetbury, but these days is mainly kept busy with ornamental work like railings and gates for homes and estates – an Iron Age blacksmith would still understand the tools he uses, he says.

So, too, techniques and tools used by master thatcher Dan Quartermain are unchanged through the centuries – the twisting of hazel spars to peg yealms (bundles) of straw into place, or using bat-like leggetts to tamp down the face of the thatch. Applied as a roof covering for thousands of years, thatch now ticks 21st-century boxes as a renewable material that provides great insulation – and Dan recycles old thatch to local farms for animal bedding.

Left: Dry stone waller Chris Ingles at work, Guiting Power.
Below: Blacksmith Richard Williams at the family forge at Cherington.

Left: Volunteers restoring a river bank.
Below: Cotswolds Conservation Board staff gathering wildflower seed.

CONSERVATION AND MANAGING NATURE RESERVES

Cotswold limestone grasslands, woods and rivers are strongholds for many rare butterflies, orchids and aquatic life, and the area's rich range of precious habitats is recognised in three National Nature Reserves (NNRs), 89 Sites of Special Scientific Interest and an excellent number of local nature reserves open to visitors.

Behind the scenes Natural England, wildlife trusts, the Cotswolds Conservation Board and a whole army of volunteers work to sustain this teeming environment.

Woodland work including the creation of glades, coppicing and the widening of rides at Avon Wildlife Trust's Browne's Folly, Bathford, has encouraged breeding birds and foraging bats – the disused quarries are home to 13 bat species including the threatened greater horseshoe – and the reserve also features the unusual Bath asparagus.

Sensitive grazing has helped to create the right conditions for the pioneering reintroduction of the once-native large blue butterfly – declared extinct in the UK in 1979 – at Gloucestershire Wildlife Trust's Daneway Banks. Ancient trees and decaying wood at Bredon Hill NNR attract over 230 species of invertebrates including the very rare violet click beetle.

Many initiatives take a 'landscape scale' approach to enhancing habitat and biodiversity, involving farmers, landowners and conservation groups in joining up activities, like pieces in a jigsaw, to maximise benefits to flora and fauna. Projects include Save our Magnificent Meadows, restoring and extending wildflower-rich grasslands, and the Cotswold Rivers Living Landscape Programme to reconnect and restore healthy river habitats: water voles, brown trout and kingfishers are among many creatures to have benefited.

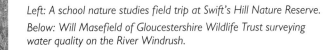

Left: A school nature studies field trip at Swift's Hill Nature Reserve.

Below: Will Masefield of Gloucestershire Wildlife Trust surveying water quality on the River Windrush.

Right: A stile at Frampton Mansell.
Opposite page: Dramatic springtime landscape at Cherington.

CARING FOR THE COTSWOLDS

The Cotswolds Conservation Board is an independent statutory organisation established in 2004 to manage the Cotswolds Area of Outstanding Natural Beauty (AONB).

The Board has two statutory purposes:

- to conserve and enhance the natural beauty of the AONB

- to increase understanding and enjoyment of the special qualities of the AONB

In fulfilling these roles, the Board must also foster the economic and social well-being of local communities within the AONB.

Working throughout the AONB are the Cotswold Voluntary Wardens; the volunteer arm of the Board. Set up in 1968, the Wardens lead guided walks and take part in a wide range of projects from dry stone walling, hedgelaying, tree planting to installing kissing gates. Their voluntary efforts are significant with contributions of over 40,000 hours of work each year.

www.cotswoldsaonb.org.uk

Landscape Character Types

The Cotswolds is a rich and varied landscape. A landscape assessment identified that the AONB comprised 19 different areas, each with its own unique landscape character.

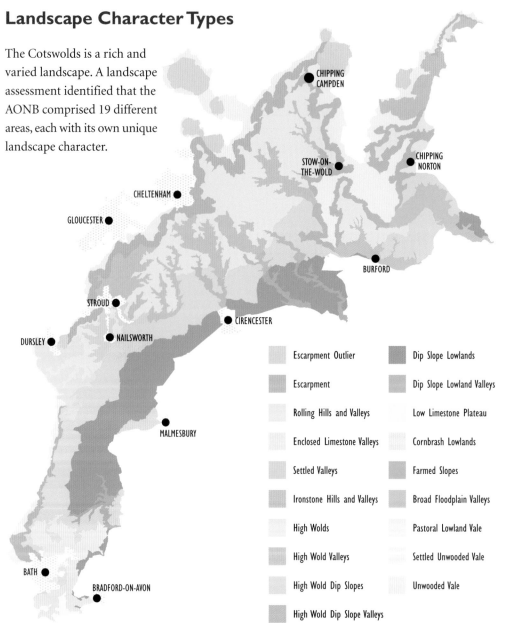

CHIPPING CAMPDEN

STOW-ON-THE-WOLD

CHIPPING NORTON

CHELTENHAM

GLOUCESTER

BURFORD

STROUD

CIRENCESTER

DURSLEY

NAILSWORTH

MALMESBURY

BATH

BRADFORD-ON-AVON

Escarpment Outlier	Dip Slope Lowlands
Escarpment	Dip Slope Lowland Valleys
Rolling Hills and Valleys	Low Limestone Plateau
Enclosed Limestone Valleys	Cornbrash Lowlands
Settled Valleys	Farmed Slopes
Ironstone Hills and Valleys	Broad Floodplain Valleys
High Wolds	Pastoral Lowland Vale
High Wold Valleys	Settled Unwooded Vale
High Wold Dip Slopes	Unwooded Vale
High Wold Dip Slope Valleys	

INDEX

CREDITS AND CONTACTS

The COTSWOLDS Area of Outstanding Natural Beauty

Design, art direction and finished artwork by
Nick Darien-Jones BA DipD of Nicholas J Jones Graphics.

Text written by Siân Ellis.

Stills and aerial photography by Nick Turner of Nick Turner Photography.

Stills equipment:
Canon 5D Mk 3 DSLR Camera, Canon 600 EX Flash, Canon 16 - 35mm F4L IS Lens, Canon 24 - 70mm F4L IS Lens, Canon 100 - 400 F4.5/5.6L IS MK 2 Lens, Sigma 150mm F2.8 Macro Lens, Sigma 50mm F1.4 EX Lens, Sigma 85mm f1.4 EX Lens, Sigma 15mm F2.8 Fisheye Lens.
Aerial equipment:
DJI Inspire 1 Quadcopter with Zenmuse X3 Camera & 20mm Lens.

Additional stills photography (Stow-on-the-Wold square, page 44; Tetbury Market House, page 45; Art Couture Painswick, page 68) and aerial photography assistance by Nick Darien-Jones.

Area map cartography (pages 12–13) by Nick Darien-Jones.

Adonis blue and Duke of Burgundy illustrations by Valerie Dugan.

Many thanks to:
Alan Sutton Publishing, Art Couture Painswick, Beaufort Polo Club, Blenheim Palace, Bourton House Garden, Ian Boyd, Carcanet Press, Simon Cooper, Cotswold Arcadians, Day's Cottage, English Heritage, Giffords Circus, The Gloucestershire Wildlife Trust, Mary Greensted, Adam Henson, Hidcote Manor, Hook Norton Brewery, Chris Ingles, Jonathan Crump Cheese, John Murray Press, Kiftsgate Court, Jessy Lee, The Lowsley-Williams family, Will Masefield, The National Trust, Overbury Estate, Steve Parkes, Bella Peralta, Dan Quartermain, Real World Music, Ian Shearman, Society of Antiquaries of London, Syreford Quarry, Westonbirt, The National Arboretum and Richard Williams.

This project would not have been possible without the support and encouragement of the Cotswolds Conservation Board (Martin Lane, Nicola Greaves, Mark Connelly and Chris Brant).

Cotswolds Conservation Board
Fosse Way · Northleach · Gloucestershire GL54 3JH
Tel: 01451 862000 · Fax: 01451 862001 · Email: info@cotswoldsaonb.org.uk

Cotswolds
Area of Outstanding
Natural Beauty